Finding Our Wordly Place

This book
belongs to:

_____

Check out our other adventures on our website:
https://phonicsadventures.my.canva.site/

Have ideas for Miss Jill's next great phonics journey? Reach out!
Instagram: @phonicsadventures
Email: phonicsadventures@gmail.com

"Words won't end with i, v, u, or j – that's a rule we'll follow every day.

Stick to it and you'll see, English words end differently!"

Once upon a time in Alphabetia, there lived a group of letters who loved to play and explore. Among them were i, v, j, and u. They were good friends, always sticking together like peas in a pod.

One day, while playing hide and seek at Letterland school, they stumbled upon a mysterious book buried high up in the library.

It was a forgotten book filled with secrets about the rules of the English language.

Curious, they opened the book and read about a strange rule.

"Words won't end with i, v, u, or j – that's a rule we'll follow every day.

Stick to it and you'll see, English words end differently!"

"What does this mean?"

"It means there are no words that end with us!"

U and v exchanged worried glances. "But why?" u wondered. V let out a sigh.

Determined to uncover the truth, the four friends embarked on a quest to find out why there were no English words that could end with them.

Their journey took them through forests of consonants, across rivers of digraphs, through vowel valley, until they reached the great Grammar Mountain, where the wise Grammarian dwelled...

"Excuse us, mighty Grammarian," said i, bowing respectfully. "We seek your wisdom. Why can't any English words end with us?"

The Grammarian smiled kindly. "Ah, young letters that is because of a special rule called the Phonics Law. Here let me show you."

The letters listened intently as the Grammarian explained the rule.

In English, words can sound like /i/, /u/, /v/, and /j/ at the end, but they can't be spelled with their letter name.

Instead, they have to change their letter(s) while keeping their sounds or add a silent e to avoid being at the end.

With this newfound knowledge in hand,
the letters started making their way back
to Alphabetia, feeling enlightened.

During their journey back, they began to
observe words in which they heard their
sounds but didn't see their letters.

Letter **j** excitedly noticed that bridge spelled his sound at the end, even though his letter wasn't used; he felt thrilled that his sound made it to the end of the word!

As day slowly turned to night, letter  u noticed letter **z** strolling through the forest. It dawned on her that zebra ended with her sound but the ending letter was changed.

Letter i looked up at the sky and realized that even though the last letter in sky didn't look like him, it still ended with his sound!

When the letters returned back to school, they were so excited to apply the knowledge the Grammarian gave them. Letter v was sad she didn't find any words that ended with her sound.

Looking back on that moment, v quickly noticed the word gave ended with her sound but recognized that it needed silent e to prevent her from being at the end and following the rule.

"We may not be at the end of words, but we are still important!" declared **j** proudly.

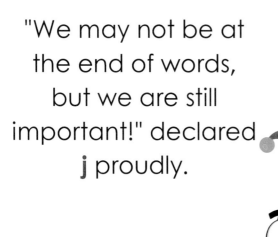

judge

huge

page

have

brave

above

"Indeed!" agreed **v**. "We help create countless words, even if we don't get to finish them."

"Our job is to help make sure words look correct and stay in the middle!" said U.

blue
few
banana

high
pie
my

"We all need help sometimes, and there's no one better than our friends to help our sounds stand strong." said i, thoughtfully.

From that day forth, i, v, j, and u embraced their role in the English language, knowing that even though they couldn't end words, they were still essential in shaping them.

And so, with hearts full of wisdom and friendship, the letters continued to play and explore, spreading the magic of language throughout Alphabetia.

Can you spy all of the words that end in /i/, /j/, /u/, /v/ in this story?

high   judge   banana
strange   huge   pie
why   page   my
sigh   brave
lived   above
have   blue
change   few

English Word Endings

"Words won't end with i, v, u, or j - that's a rule we'll follow every day.

Stick to it and you'll see, English words end differently!"

English has borrowed words from various languages over time, and they often retain their original spellings and pronunciations. Additionally, English underwent significant changes throughout its history, including influences from Old English, French, Latin, and other languages, leading to inconsistencies in spelling and pronunciation. As a result, some words have maintained their original forms despite not conforming to certain phonetic patterns in modern English. These exceptions show the rich and complex history of the English language.

Exceptions:

ski, menu- borrowed from other languages
hi - informal greeting
you thou - Old English

Made in United States
Troutdale, OR
11/06/2024